Encourage

Yourself

Hermelinda Marcos Ramos

Table of Contents

Acknowledgment 1

Dedication 5

You Are Not Alone 6

This Is Not Your Destiny 8

Set New Goals 13

Surround Yourself With Godly People.... 15

Embrace The Season You Are In.............. 18

Scriptures For Your Freedom and
Encouragement... 22

Acknowledgment

My name is Hermelinda Marcos Ramos, and I was born in Guatemala. At the age of 15 years old God led me to leave my country, family, and friends. I left my country without a plan, dreams, or goals not knowing what was on the other side. I was alone and had no family or friends to welcome me.

Because I did not have any family in the USA, and being I was a minor by God's orchestrated plan of grace and mercy the government took care of me. During this time I was going from different governmental agencies, to foster families and this was not easy for me. Sometimes these experiences made me feel like I was living in jail.

For example, I lived in two foster homes while being switched to three different government agencies simultaneously, moving nine different times to nine different places within four years. God has truly been my Father and my restorer.

God has been my inspiration throughout my time here in America. Though, encouraging myself sometimes felt like I was sewing my own wounds. This journey has been very painful and extremely sad, but through my faith in Jesus, I knew that I was going to overcome it because I had and I have The Lord Jesus Christ helping me always.

Since the beginning of my journey I told God to do His will and not mine even though my days more often than not felt like years, and the years felt like an eternity.

I started to realize that the season that I was in was not my destiny and that God was going to give me a way out. I strongly believed He would gift me with friends, family, and my purpose, and that is exactly what He did!

Dedication

This book is dedicated to my Father and my King, JESUS CHRIST, and Holy Spirit who is my inspiration, strength, life, and breath who has helped me and chosen me, and trusted me with this assignment of sharing His works within me.

I would like to honor my sister and Prophetess Jalisa Lucas who God has placed in my life to help me throughout the assignments that God has given me.
All glory be to Jesus Christ.

You Are Not Alone

Whether you believe in Jesus or not there will be many trials in your life that make you feel alone and sometimes it leads to depression. In spite of that reality, you do not have to go through it alone because you can do it with God's help and guidance.

Pain and process are necessary for our lives because it gives us wisdom while making us stronger, and transferring God's knowledge. With that being said, It does not mean that we are going to be suffering our entire lives.

"And we know that all things work together for good to them that love God, to them who are the called according to his purpose."

(Romans 8:28 KJV).

The Bible says in John 16:33, "In the world, ye shall have tribulation: but be of good cheer; I have overcome the world."

This scripture is one of my favorites, it reminds me that Jesus already died for me and He has overcome sadness, depression, loneliness, oppression, and all. It reminds me that the only thing I need to do is to be courageous, to resist the devil for him to flee from me and that remember I will have victory in the end through Jesus Christ.

This Is Not Your Destiny

This season of misery will not last long unless you want it to. I remember when the government placed me in a single-gendered (allgirls) house in Pittsburgh Pennsylvania, this house was for kids who were waiting to be reunited with their families and for those who did not have a family.

I remember so clearly how forsaken I felt during my time at the single-gendered home. Many experiences of restriction were my daily routine. For example, I was not allowed to look/see through any windows due to governmental safety policy, or even talk to anyone about my personal issues.

In addition, we were unable to physically hug one another, receive any affection or hugs from the staff, go to the bathroom alone, or even go for walks by ourselves.

Furthermore, I was not able to release my emotions such as crying without staff recording the event and assigning a therapist to ask a plethora of invasive questions that I did not have the strength to answer.

For me, the time spent in this home felt endless. I desperately wanted to reunite with my family every second of my days. During this lengthy time period I did not have anyone to encourage me, hug me or show me any affection by default, I often felt like I was walking dead. In addition to that thought, every night I use to get on my knees and cry in silence in caution due to close monitoring done by security outside my bedroom. In my desperation to be free from the emotional and psychological bondage that came with these policies, I would talk to God daily saying, "God give me strength and courage to encourage myself because I cannot do this, I need your help."

In faith for Jesus's help I would consist-
ently go to sleep knowing that God was
going to help me get through, and that I
would come out victorious and HE did!

The bible says in Jeremiah 29:11,"For I
know the thoughts that I think toward
you, saith the Lord, thoughts of peace,
and not of evil, to give you an expected
end."

What God is saying here is even though
you are going through a difficult process
he is working and thinking differently to
surprise you, to give you peace in this
time. God is not thinking like you because you are thinking; "I will drown!"

"I have no strength!" "I have no happiness!"

"I have no way out!" But God is thinking; "For you there is peace, freedom, happiness, and strength!" Amen.

Set New Goals

When going through trials in your life setting new goals and being consistent will help you to get motivated and focus your mind on things that do not bring sadness or worrying but brings you joy and new perspective about your life.

Setting new goals does not mean avoiding whatever you are going through, it means that instead of giving the problem power you use the time to heal and to withdraw yourself from pain little by little entering into your freedom.

As for me, while going into any challenging transitions in my life I always create new goals and new schedules to stay focused on because it helps me to heal quicker and not to drown in sadness and loneliness. The Bible talks about, "pressing toward the mark" in Philippians 3: 1-21 (I encourage you to read this on your own) verse 14 says, "I press toward the mark for the prize of the high calling of God in Christ Jesus."

When you start working on your new goals it can be difficult at times because of the pain but remember what your goal is and that will help you to move forward.

Surround Yourself With Godly People

Surround yourself with Godly people that will add to your life be careful not to surround yourself with people that will make you feel worthless. Many times in my life people have often tried to make me feel worthless and useless, but I would not invest my time to pay much attention or force a resolve in those situations. However, discouraging words will always have a goal to convince you that lies are the truth. As I have learned to be still in God by sitting and praying to Him while being in His presence I often asked God for strength. Sooner than later, those discouraging words and lies intended to harm me did not hurt me for much longer. Even now, God is all we need to keep going! As believers of Christ and even unbelievers It is very important to surround yourself with people who have God in their heart because they will encourage you and help you when you need it most. Godly friends are there to pray and have faith when you do not have the strength. In Ecclesiastes 4:9-12 says, "Two are better than one; because they have a good reward for their labor for if they fall, the one will lift up his fellow: but woe to him that is alone when he falleth; for he hath not another to help him up". Personally, it was very hard to find good friends however, God gifted me with very good friends since I have been in America that have been blessings to my life. In intensely difficult moments they help me to keep going which is much easier than doing it alone.

Embrace The Season You Are In

Every season in our lives teaches us something very powerful. For example, being away from my family has taught me to value and honor them even more than before and to value my time with friends and show appreciation. I remember my family back home would not make a habit of expressing much affection. We did not use words like, "I love you!"

"I am proud of you!" or "I miss you!" But being away from them, I learned to say and express my affection and speak about how much I love and miss them. Another example is my time spent while being at the single-gendered home where I was closely monitored all the time. I was not able to enjoy and do things on my own in turn, this helped me to be more grateful when I had freedom. My experiences have helped me to value more of what God has given me such as; the air, trees, sun, flowers, food and much more. As of today, I am very grateful for that season of my life because it has taught me some-thing, if I would have not gone through trials and tribulations I would have never understood the depth of what being *grateful* truly means.

"Remember every season is preparation for your next season."

-Hermelinda Marcos Ramos

Every day is different, and you need to be prepared for what that will mean for your life.

For the word of God says, "To everything there is a season, and a time to every purpose under the heaven."

(Ecclesiastes 3:1)

Be encouraged to read the Bible and speak scriptures that can inspire and help you to have strength when you need it. Always remember to be consistent in speaking life over yourself, speaking the opposite of sadness, oppression and depression. For example, "I have joy!" "I have a sound mind!" "I am loved!" "I am capable!" "I can do it!"

One more thing I want you to remember, let go and release people, things, sadness and all those memories that cause you to believe the lies of worthlessness and use-lessness. Do not be afraid to let it go. Know that in God's eyes you are more than beautiful, you are His! God will never forsake you but, it will be your de-cision to take action. Changes in your life will come when you choose life.

There is no good reason to stay in a cave of darkness, it is not worth it for you to stay bound, take your rightful place to-day and shine and walk by faith in Christ, in Jesus Name! Amen.

Scriptures For Your Freedom and Encouragement

1. (Deuteronomy 31:6) "Be strong and of a good courage, fear not, nor be afraid of them: for the Lord thy God, he it is that doth go with thee; he will not fail thee, nor forsake thee."

2. (2 Chronicles 32:7) "Be strong and courageous, be not afraid nor dismayed for the king of Assyria, nor for all the multitude that is with him: for there be more with us than with him"

3.   (Philippians 4:13) "I can do all things through Christ which strengthened me."

4.   (Deuteronomy 20:4) "For the LORD your God is he that goeth with you, to fight for you against your enemies, to save you."

5.   (2 Thessalonians 3:3) "But the Lord is faithful, who shall establish you, and keep you from evil."

6.   (Psalms 46: 1) "God is our refuge and strength, a very present help in trouble."

www.ingramcontent.com/pod-product-compliance
Lightning Source LLC
Chambersburg PA
CBHW040118150726
48005CB00013B/1774